Embracing and Anchoring Change

Seize your moment

© 2021

Philip B. Terry-Smith, Ph.D., Th.D., LCPC

www.coachpositive.com

www.drpterrysmith.com

ISBN: 978-0-9885429-6-9

9 780988 542969

Table of Contents

Introduction

Throughout your life, you will encounter many phases, many people, many jobs, and many changes. Those changes either come from within or when someone else makes a decision that causes us to make a decision about how we will or will not adjust. More often than not, in those situations, we often feel we don't have a choice. You get a job offer from a company in a new city, so you must move. Your child is struggling in school, so you need to spend more time to work with them on their studies. You come to terms with the problems in your marriage, and you have no choice but to put an end to it. In each of these situations, you may feel you have little choice. But, as we will discover, we do make the decision to pivot. Either we take the job, or we decide we don't want to uproot the family, so we keep up the job hunt.

You're here because you're ready for a change, but you're not quite sure how to commit to a new life. "Pivot" shouldn't be a scary word, and change shouldn't be a foreign concept. Why? Because it's in our nature to change regularly— we just don't realize it.

So, if you're contemplating a significant change in your life or you just made one, you're in the right place. We all have varying levels of comfort with change, and most of us are pretty reluctant to embrace it. Does that sound like you? If so, it's totally understandable.

Change isn't something that can be taught. It's person-dependent, and pivoting your life really is just a byproduct of all the events and things leading up to that point. But it's easier said than done, and it's fair that you may be cringing at the thought of changing up your current lifestyle.

This book will open your eyes to the concept of change. It will not change your mind or teach you; It will simply give you a different perspective. It will tell you why it is hard and why people struggle with it, and we will counter that with the multitude of benefits that come along with a life pivot. Then we will get to the good stuff, including when you should make a change, how to make a change, and creating patterns and everyday routines to help sustain your change(s).

So, buckle up and get ready for a new perspective—changing times are upon us!

Change

What is Change?

It's a six-letter word, both a noun and a verb, and an idea that either scares you or thrills you. Whether you thrive in new situations or you try to avoid them at all costs, you must try to get comfortable with the concept of change— because it's not going away any time soon. Better yet, you should get to a point where you understand HOW to change your life gracefully and strategically.

By definition, change means the act or instance of making or becoming different. If you're thinking, "That seems pretty hard to define," you're right. By its very nature, change is hard to characterize because change is always changing. That's mind-blowing, right? This is exactly why so many people fear change—it's the unknown, and most humans aren't comfortable with the unknown.

In the context of your life, change is broken down into different stages. It isn't instantaneous, nor is it experienced the same way for every person, so to understand what it means to you, let's look at the five stages of experiencing change:

1. **Precontemplation**—In the first stage of changing or pivoting your life, you're in denial. You don't think you need to make a change, or you're not really prepared to make one yet.

2. **Contemplation**—This stage is when you decide something needs to change. You may not necessarily be ready for the change, but you know something needs to be different. More times than not, the contemplation stage is when you realize

you will need to take on this challenge on your own.

3. **Preparation**—At this point, you've not only acknowledged that you want to make a change, but you've also decided that you will. You may not have a game plan for how you will make these changes, but you are committed to the pivot.

4. **Action**—This is the exciting stage when you're starting to put things into high gear. You're making changes and taking action to ensure that your life is pivoting. You're on the path to success!

5. **Maintenance**—This stage is often underappreciated, but it's critical to the success of your new lifestyle. In order to keep things afloat, you need to keep up with the changes you've implemented in

your life. You may experience some setbacks, and that's okay. The important thing is that you keep tracking with your goals and the changes you've implemented in your life.

If you're feeling overwhelmed by looking at these stages, don't worry. Everything has a process in life, and change is no different. Making a pivot in your life doesn't mean you need to follow a strict process. The stages above are simply listed so that you understand that you shouldn't expect a significant life pivot to happen immediately. You'll be able to relate to these steps and better understand what your mind is going through as you pivot your life.

Why Do We Struggle with It?

Think about the quote, "Change is the only constant." It sounds like an oxymoron, right? After all, if change is the only constant... doesn't that mean that nothing is consistent? If you're thinking this way, you're on the right track.

Change is omnipresent—everything and everyone is always changing. We can't keep track of changes, which makes us nervous because it means we're consistently operating within the unknown. We'll let you in on a secret (that you probably already know): Humans don't like the unknown. In addition to that, here are a few other reasons why we struggle with change:

1. It's risky
Let's face it—when we change something up, we don't know what to expect. The outcome could either be better than our starting point or

worse. That's a big risk! Think about people who change their hairstyles all the time. They're taking a risk that they may not love their new 'do, but on the flip side, there's a good chance they'll find the perfect look by testing out something different. The risk element can be scary, but we shouldn't view it as an obstacle— just something that we can work on.

2. We Lack Purpose

It's one thing to make a change; it's another to have a purposeful quest towards a life pivot. If you set out to make a change, that's exactly what you'll do. But there's no guarantee that you'll maintain or enjoy it. On the other hand, if you start with a "why," your change will have purpose and strategy—which, in the long run, leads to adherence and commitment.

3. The Changes are Unrealistic

A classic example is New Year's Resolutions. The first week of January, the gyms are crowded, people are significantly more friendly, and everyone is on their A-game at work. But after a few short weeks, everything is back to normal. In this case (and many other cases), people have a hard time implementing changes because they're setting up unrealistic expectations for themselves. If you want your life changes to stick, keep them realistic, measurable, and purposeful.

***

Humans like stability. In fact, we crave it. The reason we struggle with change is that it's a neurological imperative to be kept safe. Our primal brain is wired to crave safety and security to help us survive. When we start to step out of our comfort zone, we hear a little voice in our head telling us it's too risky. We can't do it. What if we fail? So, as you begin to make changes, even small ones, expect and accept that there will be self-doubt and fear come up. It's just your brain trying to keep you safe.

No matter how open to risk you are or how much you crave spontaneity, you—like everyone else—feel most comfortable with stability. Before you start trying to prove that you're not in favor of a stable life, let's look at a few examples that show just how extreme this principle goes. In other words, it encompasses everyone and every situation.

Example 1: Sandra is a freelance graphic designer. She loves what she does, and she grew up under the notion that passion was more important than pay. Things change when she begins to really struggle with money. She has to pick up a second job, rarely sees her family, and is always stressed out.

> **The change**: Sandra would've never envisioned herself saying this before, but she decides she wants to pursue a more

stable career path. She decides that she can always do graphic design in her spare time but that a steady paycheck sounds like the best option for her. She made a change that would have scared her just months ago, but after a series of life events, she decided it was best, and she pivoted her life for the better.

Example 2: Josh doesn't like to exercise. It has never been a big part of his life, and he gets bored as soon as he hops on the treadmill. There's a part of him that is nervous about exercising. It's intimidating to work out around other people who are experienced and comfortable with working out. For him, stability means sitting at home and watching his favorite TV show with his wife.

> **The change:** After a check-up with the doctor, Josh realizes he needs to adopt a more active lifestyle. This wasn't in the cards for him a few months ago, but his

doctor's visit catalyzes a shift. He knows that he'll feel a little unstable or uncomfortable at first, but he also knows that it's best for him—and his mindset shifts accordingly.

Example 3: Artie works at a grocery store, and he loves his job. He's friends with all his coworkers, he gets discounts on food, and he was just recently named employee of the month. For him, it's stable, and it's dependable. He has never thought about changing his job or moving to a new city because he knows there's no guarantee that he would like it.

> **The change**: One day, everything changes. He walks into work and decides he wants to do something else and experience a new environment. He doesn't know where he will go or what he will do, but this change of mind is compelling enough to encourage him to do it quickly. Artie realizes that stability,

although nice, is never a guarantee. He could lose his job tomorrow and would still be faced with uncertainties. He's now ready to take on a new environment and a new challenge.

All these examples are pretty different from each other. One of them may resonate with you... or maybe none of them do! The vital thing to note with each of these examples is that life is never a guarantee. Stability and certainty are nice-to-haves, but they are not a rite of passage. As humans, we have to embrace that change will happen, and sometimes, we need to catalyze that change.

The next time you struggle with change, remind yourself that it is 100% normal. Remember that it's just your brain's way of keeping you alive, so the species survives. In order to continue progressing and evolving, we need to be able to not only embrace change but enact it.

Now that you know what change really is, how change pertains to you, and why we, as humans, struggle with it, it's time to talk about the positives. Why is transformation necessary? What benefits does it have on your life? How will it impact you in a positive way? We'll answer all those questions and more.

Why is Change Important?

If you're reading this with a "What's in it for me?" attitude, you are not alone. We rarely associate change with positivity, but you probably do associate change with impact. Think about it logically: If things remain the same, there is no impact. Envision a diagram with a straight horizontal line. That is life without change. Sure, you may minimize the risks, but you also minimize the successes. With that in mind, here are some reasons why change is important and impactful.

1. Personal Growth
Just like flowers need water to grow, you need change to grow. With change comes learning and personal growth opportunities that will challenge you as a person for the better. You'll be pushed out of your comfort zone in the best way possible.

2. Confidence

Do you know that feeling you get when you overcome an obstacle, and you are over-the-moon happy with yourself? That's a healthy dose of confidence that you will get when you pivot your life. You'll be able to look back on all the challenges you overcame and the great things you did, and you'll celebrate. That confidence is priceless, and it is inevitable with life pivots and transitions—especially when you tackle it all on your own.

3. Motivation

Motivation is contagious. It starts with one small win, and soon enough, you can't get enough of it. In the context of changes in life, motivation will come much easier to you because you will know what you're looking for. You'll have more aim, and you'll be so much more excited about potential pivots in your life. It starts with a big one, and lucky for you, you're already halfway there!

4. Resilience

Resilience is a big deal, and for many, it's highly underrated. Being resilient means you won't back down or give up when life gets hard. And as you know, life isn't always easy. Being able to weather the storms that change brings, you'll naturally become stronger.

5. Excitement

We've talked about the harsh aspects of change or pivots in life, but there's a whole world of confusion that exists in the realm of transitions. Making changes in your life is exhilarating. There are new people to meet, new places to go, healthy habits to develop, and things to learn about yourself.

6. Opens the Right Doors (and Closes the Wrong Ones)

More often than not, you decide to make a change because something isn't going the way you want it to. In a way, you're trying to close a door that doesn't seem like the right one for you. When you embrace change, you commit yourself to closing all the wrong doors until you finally open the right one. We can't guarantee that it'll happen on the first try, but rest assured, you will definitely be able to move on in your life when you're committed to making changes.

7. Gives You a Story

Have you ever been asked, "What's your story?" and had a hard time answering it? That may be because you've hit a stopping point, and you are no longer a fan of your story. Your story is uniquely yours and it should be exciting, happy, and... YOU. The decision to pivot your life is a chance to rewrite your story. You're in the driver's seat here, so when you get nervous about taking a chance and mixing things up, remember that you are the writer of your own story.

8. Flexibility

Like an athlete who stretches every day, your mental bandwidth will stretch as you put yourself up to the challenge of tackling new changes. You'll become more adaptable because you will recognize that change is constant, and life is fluid. We can't just hope that things will always be the same and that things will always be comfortable. Instead, we'll learn how to be flexible when things take an unexpected turn, which will help you at work, in relationships, and on a personal level.

9. Learn Your Strengths

In addition to becoming more confident, you'll also learn a lot more about your strengths and weaknesses. Pivoting your life takes a tremendous amount of introspection, and in those periods of self-reflection and learning, you'll realize your strengths on a new level.

10. Compassion

Any time you get sucked into a routine, you become wrapped up in your own bubble. You may forget what's going on in the world or what it's like to go through a hardship. This lack of compassion often goes hand in hand with a mundane, routine lifestyle. Making a change does the opposite. It gives you an appreciation for challenges and triumphs, and it reconnects you to the human experience—the good, bad, and the ugly of it. In the long run, this compassion will help you and those around you.

When is it Time to Change?

If you've read through all` the wonderful benefits that come along with a significant life pivot, you may be antsy to implement a change (or two) in your life. On the flip side, you may be wondering how you know it's time to make a change. The big question is when. After all, it's not every day that we decide to change around our lives.

Sometimes we need a push in the right direction. Chances are, if you're in a rut or you've hit a roadblock, you may have a hard time coming to terms with the fact that a pivot is in order. Maybe you feel like you're dragging your feet, or perhaps you're sad. Maybe you've been stressed out, or you are angry at the way your life is going. In any of these circumstances, you are not yourself, so it may be hard to recognize when it's time for a change.

That's okay—we'll help you out! Read below for some telltale signs that it's time to make a change in your life.

You're Focusing on the Little Things

If you find yourself wrapped up in the details and stressing out over small things, you may need to shift your mindset. Typically, this is a sign that you're either bored with your life or unhappy about something. Stress manifests in lots of ways, and one of those ways is a focus on small things. The next time you find yourself stressing out about a dinner reservation or worrying about what you're going to wear to a party, stop and check-in with yourself. This focus on the little things may actually be a sign that you need to make a change in your life.

Jealousy is Hitting Hard

We're human, so jealousy is inevitable. Especially in a social media-driven world, we're bound to get jealous of other people's lives. But if you're at a point where you feel like you're comparing to every single person around you, it may be an indicator that you're simply unhappy with your life. This is a combination of "the grass is always greener" and "it's time to make a change," and in order to make your grass a little greener than it currently is... you need to change up the way you fertilize it.

You're Living in the Past

There are a few ways that you may be living in the past. 1) If you're constantly reminiscing on the old times and wishing you were back in that world, you're living in the past. 2) If you look back with regrets, you're living in the past. For example, you might be looking back on a decision you made that got you to your current life, and you regret it because you're not happy with the way your life is going. In either of these scenarios, living in the past is unhealthy. Today is what's in front of you, and today is all you know for sure. A life pivot may be in order if you realize you keep dwelling on yesterday.

Your Habits are Unhealthy

There are all kinds of unhealthy habits that we tend to adopt when we're not happy with our lives. Here are a few examples:

- Drinking regularly to forget your stress or life problems.
- Eating unhealthy food.
- Avoiding the gym.
- Isolating yourself away from your friends and family because you don't want to hear about their "amazing" lives compared to yours.
- Watching too much TV or escaping reality regularly.
- Stressing about small things.

Once you take a look at this list, think about it in the context of your life. In the back of your mind, you probably know that you've developed an unhealthy habit or two, but admitting that means admitting that you need to do something differently. Which is a daunting thought. On the flip side, if you don't pivot away from some of these bad behaviors, they will progress. Soon enough, you'll be dealing with much bigger problems. When you start to experience a combination of these things, it's time to figure out what needs to change.

You Experience "Sunday Scaries"

First of all, if you're familiar with the term "Sunday Scaries," you may have experienced them once or twice. That's okay, but if you're getting nervous every Sunday about the week ahead of you, it's time you figure that out. Not every week is going to be perfect, but the majority of your weeks should be good ones. If they're not, why wouldn't you want to change them so that they get better?

You're Tired All the Time

We're not supposed to be exhausted daily. Energy is something we naturally produce, and if we're not producing it, there may be a deeper-rooted problem—specifically one pertaining to your emotions and overall happiness. Pay attention to your yawns. They may be letting you know you need to pivot your life for the better!

Your Life Feels Like a Movie... a Boring One

There's a massive difference between a movie-like life and a dull movie script that your life follows a little too closely. If you feel like you're just following a script, reading off the lines lifelessly, and lacking plot twists, take some time to rethink how you're doing things. Do you really want your life to play out this way? Or do you want to start writing your own script? There's nothing like a good, healthy change of pace that will flip the script and keep you on your toes.

You're on Auto-Pilot Mode

Sometimes you're so used to a routine that you go through the motions without realizing it. Driving to the grocery store is a perfect example. You go the same route day in and day out, and when you get in the car and start driving, you don't take much time to notice the journey—you just get to the destination and call it a day. That's autopilot mode, and for a grocery trip, it's okay. But for your life? Absolutely not! You should not be living your life on auto-pilot mode. As soon as you feel like you might be guilty of this, you need to put it to an end. In this case, your change can be small— something as simple as noticing flowers when you walk by them or listening to the bustling city as you walk around it. Do whatever it takes to pay attention to the life around you, and you'll notice an immediate and huge difference.

You're Not Happy

This may seem simple, but you'd be surprised at how many people go through their lives feeling unhappy but doing nothing about it. If you're generally a miserable person, alarm bells should be sounding off in your head. You may not be able to pinpoint the source of your unhappiness, but logic tells you that whatever you're doing needs to change.

You're Indifferent

Indifference can be worse than unhappiness. If you've ever heard the quote, "Hate is not the opposite of love, indifference is," you would understand why. See, if you are indifferent, you've already passed the stage of wanting to make a change. Indifference signals a phase of being okay with whatever is handed your way— even if it's undesirable. Talk to any motivational speaker or success hero, and you'll quickly realize that this attitude will get you nowhere.

Sure, it may keep you on the same trajectory you're on, but it won't push you towards success or great happiness. The good news is you don't have to be indifferent. Indifference isn't permanent. It'll take some work and a whole lot of embracing change, but once you're able to, you'll make a huge difference in your life.

***

So, what will it be? Will you stay on the same path and always wonder if your life could be different, or will you take the risk and make the change? It may seem like a big deal right now. It may even look like a big deal 6 months from now. But in reality, life moves regardless of your movement. It will continue to go, and if you don't take the time to keep up with it and change along with it... you will miss out in big ways. That's why we're urging a pivot. That's why we're telling you that you are more than capable of changing your life. And that's why we're helping you along on your journey.

You now know that you need to make a change—whatever that change may be. The last step is the fun part... deciding how you will make the change!

How to Make a Change

It would be unrealistic to assume that you know how to pivot your life. Like anything in life, it takes time to understand how to try something new, and that's why we're going to break it down for you. Making a change doesn't have to be a chaotic process. Although each person will approach it differently, you can certainly follow a step-by-step process to ensure that you aren't wasting time, and you're pivoting in the right direction.

Set an Intention

This step is potentially the most important. Just like you set goals for work or fitness plans or a new year, you need to set goals for your transition in life. Going into a new life phase means a new set of intentions—and it's your job to line up those intentions for yourself clearly. To make it a little easier to understand, here's a breakdown of vague goals vs. clear, measurable intentions for your life pivot:

Vague: I'll start exercising more.

Intentional: To live a healthier lifestyle, I will start working out at the gym two times a week and attending a yoga class at least once a week for 6 months. If things go well, I'll reassess my goals and increase the cadence at which I exercise.

***

Vague: I want to try out a different career path.

Intentional: Because I'm not happy with my current career path, I will start freelancing on the side to try out different career possibilities. I'll do this for at least 6-8 months to get a good idea of what I like and don't like, and then I'll check in with myself to see what I like best.

Vague: I want to make my marriage better.

Intentional: I haven't been putting enough effort towards my marriage, and I want to change that. I will promise my spouse at least one date night every week, and when we have an argument, I will be more introspective and less defensive.

***

Vague: I'd love to start going on more vacations.

Intentional: I will reach out to my close friends to see who is down for a few vacations this year. Because I'd like to see the U.S. more, I'll be sure to target the West Coast and the South when I'm planning different trips.

Let Your Intentions Marinate

It's one thing to set goals and intentions for yourself, but it's another thing to really let them sink into your mind. After you set intentions for your new life, try meditating on them. That doesn't mean the classic yoga pose and an "ohm" every once and a while. There are several ways to meditate on your goals. Here are a few:

- **Keep a journal.** Document your thoughts and your progress regularly. Your journal will be a safe space for your thoughts.

- **Talk to your friends and family about your new life pivot**. In other words, make it official! As soon as you tell other people and garner support from your loved ones, you'll be much more likely to really commit to your new intentions.

- **Set aside more time for yourself.** There's nothing like a good ole day of TLC— especially when you're contemplating a life change. Whether it's a small life change like a new wardrobe or a significant change like an attitude pivot, "me time" will be essential to your success.

- **Document your intentions.** This is different from keeping a journal because this is more like a promise to yourself. This is less of an investigation of your feelings and more of a commitment—a written pledge, which is shown to make more of an impact on your overall success. It helps to pin your written promise somewhere visible, like a mirror, by the kitchen sink, or in your car.

Think About Your Obstacles

Did you read that correctly? Absolutely! Contingency plans are essential because they prevent you from feeling let down if things don't go according to your hopes and wishes. You mustn't be unrealistic with this life pivot, so be sure to think about any potential obstacles when you're making plans and setting intentions. It's never fun to think about the negatives, but it's even less fun to deal with them when they're unexpected. Get ahead of the game and list out some things that could potentially go wrong—you'll thank yourself in the long run!

Decide What is Realistic

Here's the bubble-burst for all the dreamers out there. Sometimes we come up with dreams that aren't realistic—and as much as it hurts, we need to determine which dreams are feasible and which ones are far-fetched. When you're trying to change up your life, you might start out with lots of ideas swarming around in your mind. That's normal, and it's an excellent way to jumpstart the "change it up" mentality. But once you've let your dreams run wild, you need to reel it back in with a dose of reality. To get you started, here are some questions you should mull over:

- Is this affordable? Often times, our idea of a significant change is a costly one. It might sound exciting at first, but when you crunch the numbers, you realize you're not financially prepared for this big of a life pivot. For example, if you decide you want to move across the country, but you don't have enough money for the move, you find yourself in a tough spot. In this case, you could push back the timeline so that you can still make your big move, but after a period of saving money.

- Do I really want this? It seems simple enough, but when we get caught up in dreamland, we tend to forget to ask ourselves the simple—but big— questions. This is a classic case with drastic hairstyle changes. Hairstylists often find people sitting in the salon chair, panic on their faces, asking the stylist if they really want a different hairstyle....after already having committed to it. This is one example of many, but the basic gist is that it's easy to get an idea in your mind that you really want something new or different. Yet perhaps you haven't thought about the actual change as much as you've thought about the *idea* of the change.

- What is my plan? This is actually a huge question that encompasses many others, but don't forget to acknowledge it as an important step in your process. You can't make a change without a plan, so once you've decided you really want the life pivot and that it is realistic for you, you'll need to start planning.

Set a Timeline

We're not about to tell you that change follows a linear path. It doesn't. It's messy, unpredictable, and often time-consuming, but that doesn't mean that it isn't doable. Once you've decided you want to pivot your life, you'll want to make it stick by setting a timeline. This timeline should be leaning on the conservative side and should definitely be realistic. If you set a timeframe of seeing the results from your change after 3 weeks, you're going to be discouraged when you don't see those results. Instead, set realistic expectations for yourself about the timing. You may consider not setting up a concrete "end goal," and instead just set up several timelines for mini-goals. There are many different ways to time it out—the important thing is to make sure you're managing your time well and managing your expectations better.

Keep Your Eyes on the Dream

We've talked about goals, and those are important—but what you really need to focus on is the big picture. It's not often in life that you'll hear that, so now is a great time to embrace it! The thing about pivoting your life is there is no formula for you to follow. There's also no timeline you have to adhere to. This is 100% a personal decision, and you don't have to do it a certain way because it's your own vision. Some people spend an entire lifetime pivoting their lives. It is a constant. With all of that said, it's exciting. Changing your experience is one of the few things you will have control over in your life. So when you start to get caught up in the nitty-gritty, try to zoom out and keep your eyes on the overall dream. Who do you want to be? What do you want your life to be like? How do you want to get there?

Replace Old Habits

Part of your change will be focused on pivoting toward what you do want, and part of your change will be about pivoting away from what you don't want. We're all guilty of forming bad habits throughout our lives, and when you're making changes in your lifestyle, it's a good time to start whittling down those bad habits. To make things easier, instead of trying to get rid of a bad habit, try swapping it for a better one. For example, if your habit is that you eat ice cream late at night, try swapping the ice cream for a bowl of berries. That way, you're not going cold turkey, but you're still ensuring that the bad habit is being phased out.

Stick with it

This is the hardest of them all, and you probably know exactly why. How many times have you said you would start doing something, felt really committed, and then 6 weeks later it completely stopped? Chances are, you've probably done this pretty often. We've all been there. It's hard to keep up with a change. But this one is different—it's not just a change, it's a life pivot. You're not here because you want to change the way you exercise or start eating healthy. You're here because you don't like the way you're living your life, and you're ready to shift it so that you are happier with your life. Simple enough, right? Whenever you get the feeling that you want to give up, come back to your why. Ask yourself why you decided to make this change in the first place. Remember where you were a few months ago and why you weren't happy with that version of yourself. Come back to your list of things you want to change. It may be hiding, but it's in there. It's in you.

Pivot Summary

Our advice on how to make a change was probably a lot easier than you thought it would be. Pivoting your life isn't difficult—people do it every single day.

What's hard is when you're reluctant to make the change. The good news for you is you're already there. You know you want to transition your life so that it's in a better place, you know what you need to do, and you've got a good idea of how to do it. You're already one step ahead of the game. The next step is to get to work.

Ready, set, pivot!

Part II

EVERYDAY
The Power of Daily Routine

The Power of Routine

Whether you are aware of it or not, routine plays a large part in all of our lives.

You may not currently be cognizant of your daily routines, but there is a big chance they are a significant part of your success. While on the other hand, negative routines may be unwittingly holding you back.

The dictionary defines routine as:

A sequence of actions that are regularly followed

As soon as you read that definition, you probably instantly thought of a number of routines you follow almost without thinking. These are the kind of daily actions you mindlessly take no matter what.

Most of us inherently have routines based around things like our sleep, eating, hygiene, exercise and much more. Some of these routines are good and some of them ...well not so much.

You might not think about these things as a routine per se, but by definition they really are. They are quite literally *a sequence of actions regularly followed.*

For example, almost anyone reading this probably has the same type of routine before bed every night. You go to the bathroom, you wash your face, brush your teeth, etc. No matter what specific actions you follow it is probably quite similar each evening.

That is a routine.

This guide, is all about being aware of AND harnessing the power of such routines.

Why Is Routine So Powerful?

Routine can be a powerful tool once you recognize its importance.

Having routines that you already follow everyday is great, but that is just the tip of the iceberg. When you tap into the true power of routine, and create specific repeatable actions that propel you towards your goals – that's when things get real.

The power of routine can't be overstated. Just revisit the definition mentioned on the last page....

A *sequence of actions regularly followed* is pretty much the key to succeeding at anything.

- If you want to lose weight, you need to regularly repeat certain actions like eating healthy, or exercising.
- If you want to build wealth, you need to regularly repeat the actions that help you gain and save money.
- If you want to be happy, you need to regularly repeat the actions that make you feel happy.

Healthy, wealthy and happy – that is pretty much success in anyone's eyes right?

Consciously creating routines actually makes repeating these needed actions *easier* as well.

Once you have created a routine and committed to it, quite often the actions you are repeating will become second nature.

You won't have to think about taking action, you will just do it!

On top of that, the more you do something, the better you get at it. By it's very nature, routine promotes practice.

In summary...

- Routine helps you work towards your goals
- It ***keeps*** you working towards those goals regularly
- It makes you better at the work you need to do to reach your goals

Sounds pretty powerful to me!

Why Do We Struggle with Routine?

The biggest struggle we have with routine is not recognizing its importance and/or not actively creating powerful routines in multiple areas of our life.

Most of us go about our daily lives, not fully aware of our routines. We just mindlessly repeat certain actions each day. Sometimes to our benefit, and sometimes to our detriment.

When you are aware of the concept and power of routine, you can actively try to create new powerful ones that can drastically change your life.

At the same time, awareness allows you to identify negative routines that you have fell into, and you can adjust or eliminate them. You may be repeating negative actions daily without even realizing it.

Another common struggle with routine is ability to commit to it. This is usually because of one of the following factors:

- You are creating routines that don't match your goals or passion
- You are trying to create too many routines at once
- You don't have an action plan
- You haven't read this guide ;)

What You Will Learn as we move forward

This guide is all about **routine awareness**!

We will start by sharing some stories of *massively* successful people and the routines they used to drive themselves towards their accomplishments.

Almost any success story includes some sort of routine that helped get the successful person there. I think these stories will inspire you, as well as shed more light on just how powerful routine can be.

Most importantly, we will walk you through some simple steps to help you create your own routines. These steps will be universal enough that you can apply them to any area of your life.

You will learn what to do, and what not to do when it comes to creating routines.

If you follow our simple process, you will be able to create powerful routines that propel you towards your goals.

Conversely, the general knowledge gleaned from this eBook will help you notice and rectify any negative routines in your life.

Even while reading these first few pages, you have probably already thought about a couple of negative routines that you have. Knowledge is power! Without reading another sentence, you have already taken the first step towards rectifying your negative routines.

Lastly we will share a list of 50 powerful routine examples. These routines might be things you want to incorporate into your own life right away. If not, they may inspire you to think of your own powerful examples. Either way, you will be taking your first steps toward success.

Famous Routines of Successful People

It doesn't take too much digging into success stories to find examples of powerful routines.

These routines not only help people reach their lofty peaks, they were likely quite integral to them.

Below you will find 8 stories of famous people and their routines.

We stuck to this number so we wouldn't overwhelm, but this list was whittled down from dozens. I am sure with more research it could have easily been in the 100s.

Like they say, every good success story starts with a routine! OK, they don't really say that ...but maybe they should.

The people below are all super successful in their fields, and were known to have powerful routines that were significantly important to this success. First we will quickly break down their routine (and some are deceptively simple). Then we will share the takeaway you should have gotten from the story.

Pay close attention to these takeaways, because they are powerful tips that will help you when you create your own routines.

Don't worry if you can't remember every takeaway as you read. We include a handy bulleted list at the end of this section.

Steve Jobs

"If today was the last day of my life, would I be happy with what I'm about to do today?" –
Steve Jobs

One simple question, each morning in the mirror.

The above quote is the focal point of Steve Jobs morning routine. I am fairly certain he had a number of routines, but this one is particularly fascinating.

After he would wake up, he would face himself in the mirror and ask that question. If he answered "no" too many days in a row, then he knew he had to shake things up.

Jobs knew that life was too short to waste time doing things that don't make him happy. He wanted to make sure he was doing important, fulfilling work each day.

By checking in each morning, Jobs made sure he was being true to himself and it helped keep him on his chosen path.

Your Takeaway:

What a simple, yet powerful routine. How many times do you wake up and just start getting ready for work?

How powerful would it be if you actually took a moment to ask yourself a simple question like that? A routine doesn't have to be a grand gesture, or major lifestyle change. Sometimes, something as simple as asking yourself a question every morning can help drive you towards success.

John Grisham

"The alarm clock would go off at 5, and I'd jump in the shower. My office was 5 minutes away. And I had to be at my desk, at my office, with the first cup of coffee, a legal pad and write the first word at 5:30, five days a week." **– J. Grisham**

This is probably obvious to most people, but John Grisham is a writer. He is an amazingly prolific and popular one at that. It makes sense that his routine revolved around writing. A good routine should complement your passion.

Every working day, Grisham would get up at the same time and be ready to roll at 5:30am. His goal was to **write a single page every day.**

Another simple yet powerful goal. He was a writer and his routine was... to write. It could take an hour, or it could take 5 minutes, but the routine was the same - a page a day.

With dozens of massively successful books under his belt, it is safe to say it worked.

Your Takeaway:

Making your passion part of your routine can be very powerful. If you know your passion and are actively following it, then why not create a daily routine based around it?

Another lesson to be learned from Grisham is that choosing a results based routine can be very helpful. Instead of forcing yourself to do something for X amount of time, why not focus on the result you want instead? In Grisham's case, he didn't force himself to write for 2 hours each day. Instead he set a goal of a single page with a much more flexible time frame.

Beethoven

Beethoven, one of the most successful and renowned musicians of all time, was widely known as a man of routine.

In fact, he took it to the next level in some cases. He purportedly started each morning by meticulously brewing his morning cup of coffee by counting out 60 coffee beans.

For the focus of this guide though, we want to look at his afternoon. After a morning of work and a midday dinner, Beethoven would go on a long, often vigorous walk.

The key to this walk was that he always brought a pencil and couple sheets of music paper in case he was struck with musical inspiration.

He used a change of state and environment to break up the monotony of his day, while at the same time making sure he was ready if inspiration struck.

Your Takeaway:

Create routines that help you in multiple ways. Beethoven's midday vigorous walk, while simple in it's nature, is actually complex when you look at the effect it had on him.

This one single routine, actually addressed multiple issues. A vigorous walk is a wonderful way to stay active. It is even better if you commit to it daily. On top of that, it was a great way to shake things up. A midday walk can break up the doldrums of working all day and help inspiration strike. Beethoven made sure he was ready by carrying pencil and paper.

This one routine was actually a triple threat!

Maya Angelou

"We have a semblance of a normal life. We have a drink together and have dinner. Maybe after dinner I'll read to him what I've written that day. He doesn't comment. I don't invite comments from anyone but my editor, but hearing it aloud is good." **– Maya Angelou**

Another successful writer, Maya Angelou was also a firm believer in routine. Are you starting to see a pattern here?

When she was working, she had a strict routine that she followed each and every day.

A normal working day for Angelou, would start with a 6am morning coffee with her husband. After that, they both head off to work. She would head to a sparsely furnished room where she could focus on nothing but her passion.

She would work until the afternoon (exact time depended upon how well things were going) and then meet up with her Husband for a drink and dinner together.

Your Takeaway:

The highlight in this routine is balance! Angelou works hard and focuses, everyday, but she also ensures her life has balance. In her own words, "we have a semblance of a normal life".

This is an important lesson for anyone. Sometimes we get so wrapped up in our goals and passion, that we forego life's simple pleasures. Being able to have a drink and dinner with a loved one, is something we shouldn't take for granted.

You should strive to create daily routines that honor multiple aspects of life – emotional, spiritual and physical.

Jack Dorsey

*"I look to build a lot of consistent routine, Same thing every day." – **Jack Dorsey***

Jack Dorsey might not be as universally known as some of the other people in this list, but that is definitely changing. In younger circles, he may be more popular than some of the others on this list.

Dorsey is the co-founder of tech giants Twitter and Square.

Like a lot of tech wunderkinds, he has a fairly strict daily routine that allows him to simplify certain aspects of his life.

His morning ritual is simple. He wakes up at 5am, meditates for 30 minutes, works out and then rewards himself with a caffeine fix.

This is far from a groundbreaking routine, but it has 2 key takeaways that make it worth highlighting.

Your Takeaway:

The first takeaway comes from the reasoning behind his love of routine. In the same interview where we pulled the above quote from, he went on to say that these daily **routines allowed him a measure of control** even when the rest of his day was throwing all sorts of crazy obstacles at him. Routines can be a source of calm, even in the middle of chaos.

Secondly, leaving his coffee until after his routine is finished, adds a reward to the whole concept. **His subconscious knows that if he focuses and gets his routine done, he will receive that reward** of coffee at the end. This can be motivating even if you don't consciously consider it a reward.

Stephen King

*"I have a glass of water or a cup of tea. I have my vitamin pill and my music, sit in the same seat, and the papers are all arranged in the same places. The cumulative purpose of doing these things the same way every day seems to be a way of saying to the mind, you're going to be dreaming soon." – **Stephen King**

You'd be hard pressed to think of a more prolific or popular writer than Stephen King. Like the other writers we have focused on, he also has a routine. Just like them, it isn't anything intense, it is basically all covered in the above quote.

He wakes up, gets ready and then he writes. The key for him, is the **repetition.**

He not only keeps his routine the same, **but also his surroundings**. Right down to the placement of his papers!

Again this isn't groundbreaking stuff but it illustrates an important takeaway...

Your Takeaway:

The cumulative effects of routine are what matter most. **It doesn't matter what you accomplish in one day, it matters what you accomplish at the end of a year (or longer) of those days.**

What might seem silly and simple in the moment (i.e. making sure your papers are in the same place) is in fact a mental cue that helps you maintain your routine, recapture your state of mind and repeat it each and every day.

Susan Sontag

While she may be a somewhat controversial figure to some, no one can ever doubt Sontag's accomplishments and commitment to her chosen causes.

She not only produced a massive amount of content, she was also refreshingly open about how she accomplished it.

Below is an except from her published journal (*As Consciousness Is Harnessed to Flesh: Journals and Notebooks, 1964-1980*)

> *I will get up every morning no later than eight. (Can break this rule once a week.)*
>
> *I will have lunch only with Roger [Straus]. ('No, I don't go out for lunch.' Can break this rule once every two weeks.)*

I will answer letters once a week.

This isn't her full daily routine, but I chose this excerpt because it illustrates a remarkable takeaway.

Your Takeaway:

Commitment to your routine is key, but do you see how she built flexibility into it by allowing herself a weekly rule break?

It's important to build some flexibility into your routines, so you don't feel like a failure the first time you miss a day. Commitment and repetition of routine is paramount, but don't beat yourself up if you miss a day. Real life happens.

Anna Wintour:

Anna Wintour is a massively successful journalist and editor. In fact, she has been the editor in-chief for Vogue magazine since 1988. Whether or not you are a fashionista, you should appreciate just how important of a figure she is in that world.

Like all the uber-successful people in this guide, she has a daily routine. Unlike some of the people already mentioned though, she has an interesting twist. First lets look at her morning...

6:45 AM: An hour of tennis.
7:45 AM: Has her hair blown out.
9:00AM: Ready for the day's work.

The part I love – is the hair blown out. Now, in the world of fashion, it is probably pretty important to look great. However, It's how that blow-out makes her feel that I am interested in.

A simple pleasure like getting her hair done, makes her feel ready to take on the world.

She doesn't just start her day looking great, **she starts it feeling great.**

Your Takeaway:

Embrace routines that help you feel empowered, no matter what it is. **I am actually telling you to be selfish.** All of your routines don't have to be about some greater goal. Sometimes it can be about making yourself feel happy.

Don't be afraid to embrace your personal preference when you create daily routines. You might not want to get a morning blow-out each day, but if you have a daily ritual that really helps you feel better – embrace it!

Revisiting The Takeaways

Below is a list of takeaways from the routine success stories above.

Feel free to revisit this list often. You can even print this page out, and post it somewhere to remind yourself of these tips.

Reading these takeaways daily could become your first routine!

- Simple daily routines can be powerful
- Create routines that match your passions
- Create routines that help you from multiple angles
- Create daily routines that honor multiple aspects of life – emotional, spiritual and physical
- Routines can add a level of control to otherwise chaotic days
- Build a reward directly into your routine

- The cumulative effects of routine are what matter most
- Don't fear a little flexibility in your routines
- Don't be afraid to embrace your personal preference when you create daily routines

Improve and Create Your Own Powerful Routines

In this section, we will examine some of the best practices to help you improve your current routines, as well as intentionally set new powerful ones.

These steps will be general enough you can use them to focus on multiple areas of your life.

Step One: Your Motive

Before you begin to look at your daily tasks and routines, you need to first think about what you really want to accomplish. What is the motive behind you wanting to tap into the power of routine?

The easiest way to do this, is to examine (or set) some long term goals. You should have goals that focus on the things you find important. Successful people usually have goals based around things like:

- Household
- Health/Fitness
- Work
- Family
- Spiritual
- Financial

Take some time to think about long-term goals you would like to accomplish in each of those areas. This is important, so that later on you can assure that your current routines are working towards these. Also, you will be able to create new routines that address any current areas of weakness.

Step Two: Examine Your Day

Now you want to examine what you already do on a daily basis. You may already have routines that you aren't aware of. Alternatively, you might be on the cusp of having helpful routines, and just need a nudge to get there.

To start examining your day, simply spend a day recording all the tasks you do. Start with a single day, but keep in mind recording a whole week will be significantly more helpful.

Start recording what you do when you wake up, right up until you go to bed.

- Think about the things you have to do before you go to work
- Think about everything you need to do to help your family get their day started
- Consider the repeatable tasks you need to do at work

- Consider the repeatable tasks you need to do to keep the household running (cleaning, organizing, eating, etc...)
- Ask yourself what errands you need to complete
- Ask yourself what things you do to stay in good health
- Think about the things you do for your financial health

Once you have jotted down all of your tasks, you will have a master list of the things you do already

Step Three: Examine Your List

Now that you have your list, examine it and take stock of the things you do daily.

Ask yourself the following questions about each task...

- Is this a positive or negative daily action?
- Are these actions progressing me towards my goals?
- Are these actions an efficient use of my time?

If you find a number of daily tasks that are positive, fit your goals and efficient uses of your time – highlight them.

These are powerful daily routines that you already have and you should commit to continuing and perfecting them.

Alternatively, if tasks don't tick off all the 3 above boxes, you might want to look at dropping them, or replacing them with new routines.

Step Four: Look For Weakness

Earlier you wrote down (or set new) goals that addressed a number of areas in your life. Looking at that list try and pinpoint any weaknesses in your daily tasks routines.

- Are any of your goals not being addressed properly?
- Are you doing things everyday that progress you towards each of your goals.
- Are the things you are doing, as good as they can get?

If so – then congrats you are using the power of routine already!

If not, and let's be honest, most of us can do better, then you should jot down where you think you are struggling.

Create a list of the areas that you don't do enough each day to address.

For example – some people might get a lot of exercise each day, but they aren't saving enough money. If this is you, then you would write down "financial" as an area of struggle.

At the end of this step you should have a number of areas in your life you need to focus on.

Step Five: Brainstorm New Routines

Using the list you created last step, focus on the areas of life you feel you aren't properly addressing yet. Make a list of a 2-3 things you could do each day to address them.

For example, of you highlighted "financial", go ahead and write down a daily task or two that can help you with that. The task could be something like cutting down on lunches out, or it could be throwing your loose change into a change jar at the end of each day.

Step Six: Schedule Your New Routines

Ideally after the last step, you will have a number of potential new routines you can start to incorporate into your life.

You should take some time now, to figure out how these will best fit into your life.

If you are someone who already has a day planner, and you schedule your life down to the hour – then you will simply plot these new routines where they fit.

If you are a little more flexible with your time, then you will still want to take some time to think about where these routines naturally fit into your day.

Instead of stridently scheduling them into your day, you can simply categorize them by the time of day that most makes sense. Keep it simple with 3 categories:

- Morning routines
- Afternoon routines
- Night routines

When you are separating your routines into these categories, remember to honor your own personal preference. Some people like to get more complex tasks done early, while some people like to spend their mornings in a more reflective or laid-back state.

Some people find their creative juices flow the best when they first wake up, while others like to spend their nights being creative.

The important part here is being true to yourself.

Not only do you have to be true to yourself, **you need to be true to your circumstances**. If you are rushed off your feet in the morning already, then creating a 30-minute meditation routine during that time, might not fly.

Adjust your routines to fit your personal preferences, as well as your personal circumstances. **The easier it is to fit your routine into your life, the easier it will be to stick to it.**

Speaking of which...

Step Seven: Stick To It

Simple right – just keep on doing the routine!

Wait a sec... Actually it isn't that simple. Committing to doing a new daily task, no matter how trivial, isn't just as simple as wanting to do it. If that were the case, we would all get enough exercise, save a ton of money and have a totally clean and organized house.

The truth is, committing to a new routine is much tougher than simply creating one.

To help your routine stick you should take a couple of steps:

1. **Commit to 30 days** – There is a lot of info out there claiming there is a specific timeframe to make a habit/routine stick. I don't know how true it is, but I do know that 30 days is both reasonable, and long enough to get into a pattern.

2. **Use a calendar or app to mark each day done** – There is something really powerful about seeing your progress right

in front of you. Ideally, you would get a calendar, hang it somewhere you constantly see and each day mark an X through the day you completed your new routine(s). Conversely, if you have a number of new tasks/routines you want to stick to, you could use color coded stickers.

If you want a more high-tech option, there are plenty of habit-creation apps that will also allow you to track your month of new routines. One note here though – make sure you enable notification on these apps so that you will get regular reminders. It's much easier to forget to use the app, than it is when you have a physical calendar in your face. Use the notifications to bridge that gap.

3. **Build in flexibility** – While aiming for everyday is pretty important. Let's not

forget that life happens and we need to be flexible at times.

Remember Susan Sontag? She built flexibility right into her routines when she wrote them down. She allowed herself a free rule break once a week.

If you don't like that idea, you could make up a rule that you can break your new routine for a day, as long as you don't do it again on a consecutive day.

No matter how you incorporate flexibility (and the two examples from above are hardly the only ways) you just need to figure out what works best for you.

4. **Build in a reward** – Guess who likes rewards? Everyone.

   You should try and think of a reward that you can give yourself if you go the full 30 days with your new routine(s). Try to think of a reward that really means something to you. Don't think of anything too extravagant or out of your means, just choose a single simple reward that makes you happy in the moment.

Jack Dorsey of Twitter had a simple daily reward of a cup of coffee.

You can choose something that resonates more with you, but that just goes to show you that you don't have to go overboard.

If you want to reward yourself something really exciting, and maybe a bit luxurious – try and make it match your goals.

For example, set a new routine to get more active and stick to it for a full month. If you are able to do that, you might reward yourself with a new gym membership, some nice basketball shoes or a new bike.

Those are pretty significant rewards, but they directly address your personal goals, and will quite likely help you accomplish them more efficiently.

Step Eight: Self-Reflection

Once you have reached the end of your month (ideally successfully) it is time to sit back and take some time to reflect on how it went. Ask yourself these questions:

- What went well with my new routine?
- Did my new routine have an appreciable effect on my life?
- What part of my new routine did I struggle with?
- What part of my routine did I truly enjoy?

- What could I do to make my routine more efficient?
- Is this something I want to continue?
- Is there a better use of my time?

Asking yourself these types of questions will help you correct your trajectory (if need be) and tweak your routines so that they are more helpful or efficient.

Don't be afraid to drop routines that haven't helped you, or just don't vibe with your life. On the same token, don't be afraid to double-down on routines that have had significant impact on your life, or that you love.

Step Nine: Tweak Them And Start A New 30 Days

It's a routine right? You don't stop doing it. Take what you learned from the above self-reflection and work on perfecting these new routines.

If you keep going through Steps 8 and 9 after each 30 days, you will be regularly improving your routines until they are perfect.

Your commitment to creating and perfecting routines, will actually become a routine itself!

The power of routine is a powerful force that only gets more powerful as you fully acknowledge and embrace it. Anyone who follows these 9 steps is doing both.

50 Daily Routine Examples

In this section, we are sharing some examples of routines that you could incorporate into your life. These may not seem life-changing or momentous, but focusing on just a few of them will help you build positive routines that help you reach your goals.

If you are interested in any of these, I would caution you to focus on only a few at a time. Also, try to choose routines that match your goals. Feel free to tweak the below routines to fit those goals as well.

Not every routine below will mention "everyday" or "each day" but that's the whole point of a routine. If we give an example that doesn't specifically mention everyday, assume that's what it means.

1. Create a personal daily hygiene routine
2. Get dressed to impress each morning, even if you work from home
3. Drink 8oz of water as soon as you wake up
4. Eat a healthy protein packed breakfast before you head out for the day
5. Spend some time each night thinking about what you are grateful for
6. Every night before bed, write down some key to-dos for the next day
7. Spend some time meditating
8. Spend 5 minutes each morning scheduling your day
9. Make a goal to save X amount of money daily
10. Reach out to a new networking connection
11. Read and visualize your long-term goals

12. Find an exercise activity you'd love to do

13. Find a hobby that you can dedicate time to

14. Set a step goal, and hit it

15. Make a habit of reading something inspirational

16. Make a habit of reading something educating

17. Have a go-to song (or playlist) that pumps you up in the morning

18. Make your bed when you get up

19. Start practicing yoga, stretching or foam rolling

20. Do something nice for someone else

21. Do something that makes you happy

22. Make it a priority to talk with happy or positive people

23. Get out into nature

24. Practice deep breathing for a few minutes

25. Listen to something calming

26. Reach out to a close friend

27. List three great things about yourself

28. Write down one major thing you want to accomplish that day

29. Ask yourself if you are doing something you are proud of

30. Find a mantra, and repeat it for a few minutes

31. Step outside your comfort zone and try something that challenges you

32. Turn off all of your devices for a set period of time

33. Take a risk (big or small)

34. Tidy your workspace, and prepare it for the next day

35. Answer your emails at a set time

36. Smile and/or laugh

37. Do something that makes you feel beautiful

38. Do something that makes you feel powerful

39. Do something that makes you feel confident

40. Eat something healthy that you might not like that much

41. Set and achieve a micro-goal

42. Check in with a mentor or accountability buddy

43. Go to sleep at the same time

44. Create a bed time ritual

45. Commit to waking up earlier than usual

46. Use the morning to plan your meals for the day

47. Try something new

48. Take a meaningful break from work

49. Study your finances/spending

50. Start keeping a journal

Conclusion

Routine plays a massive role in all of our lives –
whether we are aware of it or not.

Everyone reading this has some sort of routine
in their life. If you read the list of example
routines from the last chapter, you can probably
tick off more than a couple that you already go
about daily without barely knowing it.

That's why routine can be so powerful! When
you commit to routines that align with your
goals, eventually these actions will become
something you do without thinking about it. You
will be attacking your goals every single day
almost mindlessly.

You have also learned about how powerful
routine was in the lives in some seriously
successful people.

On top of that, you have seen how they used fairly simple routines to reach their lofty goals. That's the great thing about routine. We don't need to smash it out of the park each and every day. We just chip away daily, and the cumulative power of doing that can add up to great things.

You also learned how you can start intentionally creating new routines that will help propel you to your own goals. The steps included here are general enough that you can start creating routines across multiple aspects of your life right now.

If you need some inspiration, check out the examples we shared a few pages ago.

Out of those examples, you can find at least one or two to start on right away. If not, just reading them could inspire you to think up your own original routines.

What are you waiting for? Its time that you let the power of routine take control and help rocket you towards your best life!

EMBRACE Your change, Anchor, Build routines and Seize the Moment.

~ PBTS

www.ingramcontent.com/pod-product-compliance
Lightning Source LLC
La Vergne TN
LVHW011408080426
835511LV00005B/431